World Class Mulligans
For Golfers With Extra Balls

To Larry!

Got Balls?

Andy Pavzit

7.22.18

World Class Mulligans
For Golfers With Extra Balls

Golf Mulligan Association
Official User's Guide

Andy Parzit

NooVoo Publishing

World Class Mulligans and Golf Mulligan Association are
trademarks of NooVoo Publishing LLC

All of the characters in this book are fictitious and any
resemblance to actual persons, living or deceased, is purely
coincidental.

ISBN 0-9767513-0-5

Printed in the United States of America

Library of Congress Control Number: 2005924451

For information contact:

NooVoo Publishing LLC
28257 Thorny Brae Road
Farmington Hills, Michigan 48331
or
Email: info@noovoo.com

This book is available at quantity discounts at:

www.WorldClassMulligans.com

Dedication

To all golfers who want to improve their scores and need a 100% guaranteed way to get the job done.

Warning

If you are already experiencing personal problems associated with golf, you should exercise caution when using this guide. Mulligan addiction is a common side effect.

Contents

World Class Mulligans
Introduction

Welcome! I am Andy Parzit, Director of Public Relations for the Golf Mulligan Association. <u>World Class Mulligans</u> is the official mulligan user's guide of the Association. Whether you received this guide as a gift, purchased it for yourself, or stole it from someone else's golf bag, you are in for a real treat. This landmark publication is changing the face of golf.

The golf mulligan, or takeover golf shot, is used worldwide by golfers to improve their scores. Based on official estimates, a golfer is taking a mulligan about once every second somewhere in the world. Mulligans range from the standard, pre-approved "first tee reload" to the very extreme mulligan mutation: "I can't find my ball – oh, I suddenly found my ball" (executed cleverly using the provisional pocket ball).

The official rules of golf have not permitted the use of mulligans and, as a result, every golfer has experienced some level of guilt using one. My friends, I have very good news for you. This will not be the case in the future because I am pleased to announce the formation of the Golf Mulligan

Association, and to inform you that we have sanctioned and approved the use of mulligans for the game of golf.

The United States Golf Association (USGA) and other "golf police" will be very angry about our bold move to sanction and approve the use of mulligans. You should not be concerned. We don't care one divot about what they think and they are powerless to do anything about it!

With this Official User's Guide you will become an expert user of the golf mulligan and you will see a dramatic improvement in your golf score overnight. More important, you will do this with a guilt-free conscience because you will be using the official, sanctioned, world class mulligans included in this guide.

To help you make a quantum improvement in your golf scores, we provide all of the necessary tools:

1. **Psychological Conditioning** – When we get done with you, you will never feel guilty about taking a mulligan as long as you live.

2. **Membership in the Association** – All you need to do is participate in some golf related shenanigans later in this guide to

get a free lifetime membership in the Association.

3. **World Class Mulligans** – We supply an arsenal of the finest reasons to retake a golf shot! You're going to love these! (Pardon me if I am getting a little too enthusiastic. I get very excited when I talk about the subject of world class mulligans.)

4. **Assistance for Addicts** – If you have personal problems associated with mulligan abuse, or golf in general, we provide you a unique method of coping.

You should keep this guide with you at all times when you are golfing. If you, a friend, your golf foursome, or your golf outing want to improve their scores, this guide is a guaranteed way to get the job done.

To begin your journey the President of the Golf Mulligan Association, Moe Strokes, will give you a brief introduction to the Association.

Hit 'em good or hit 'em over! – Andy Parzit

The Golf Mulligan Association

President
Moe Strokes

The Golf Mulligan Association

Future members, and soon to be good friends, I am Moe Strokes, President of the Golf Mulligan Association. In the next few pages I will introduce you to our philosophy and the people who make it happen here at the Association. (I am so proud of our team!)

One thing that will become apparent as you review the next few pages is the Association's clear sense of direction and purpose. The world class mulligans that are included in this guide directly reflect the strength of our team and their dedication to carrying out the mission of the organization.

Background

The Golf Mulligan Association is an ultra-modern, hi-tech, fictitious organization. We have no facilities, membership fees, or annual picnics. I am not a real person and neither are any of the people, places, or things mentioned in this guide. That said, if you are really open-minded and "hip", you will just jump in your golf cart and get with the program.

The Golf Mulligan Association and the idea to sanction and approve golf mulligans were the pure genius of our founder, Howard Takovar. Previously, Howard was the head of accounting for a major company. In that capacity he was frequently pressured to "help the bottom line". He left the company because this conflicted with his personal ethics. Then, he began work on something that he was more comfortable with - the golf mulligan.

As a 30 handicap golfer with corporate experience, Howard had both the motivation and skills to develop what has now become an internationally recognized golf essential; the Golf Mulligan Association approved mulligan. His work is legendary among desperate, struggling, and forlorn golfers – just like you.

Howard was tragically taken from us in a bizarre golf related accident that involved a poorly hit five iron, a drunken golfer, a divot tool, a hot dog, and a deep pond. The details are not appropriate subject matter for this guide.

Before his untimely demise, Howard built the foundation for the Association. His important contributions include writing our organization's mission statement, developing our motto, creating a vision, and hiring a staff of key people with the talent and motivation to make it all happen.

Our Mission

We will provide golfers a 100% guaranteed way to reduce their golf scores without the need for additional lessons, equipment purchases, driving range visits, score card changes, or other humiliation.

Our Motto

"Colpiscono la palla buona o colpiscono la palla ancora" *

* Translation: They hit the good ball or they hit the ball again. ("Hit 'em good or hit 'em over!").

Our Vision

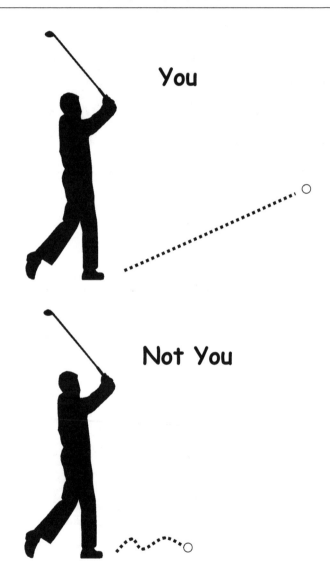

You

Not You

Our Vision

You

Not You

Our Vision

You

78

Not You

112

Our Vision

You

Not You

Our Vision

Our People

President
Moe Strokes

Experience: Former Supervisor of Covert Operations for the Central Intelligence Agency. A promising professional golfer who failed to get his tour card after 17 attempts. A solid combination of dangerous and pissed off.

Director of Public Relations
Andy Parzit

Experience: Carnival sideshow barker, freshman psychology professor, and ambulance chasing attorney. Worked for ten years writing public relations material for the tobacco and asbestos industries.

Our People

Director of Membership and Training
Pat Faraway

Experience: Timesharing condominium sales manager (Voted #1 for six consecutive years). Developed the membership programs for several of the nation's prominent record, movie, magazine, and fruit-of-the-month clubs.

Director of Mulligan Research
Ben Whiffin

Experience: Former priest, IRS Agent, parole board member, and golf driving range manager. Has heard every form of an excuse that can possibly come from a human being.

Our People

Director of Member Assistance
U.T. Upagain

Experience: Former manager of the Clinic for General Addictive Disorders in Melville, Ohio. Author of the best seller: Drinking, Gambling, Sex, and Staying Out Late in Moderation.

Now that you have an understanding of our organization and the hardworking people that make it all possible, we can get on with making you a member of the Association. In the next section, Pat Faraway, our Director of Membership and Training, will guide you through the process.

Hit 'em good or hit 'em over! – Moe Strokes

Becoming a Member

Director of Membership and Training

Pat Faraway

Becoming a Member of the
Golf Mulligan Association

Introduction

Hi, my name is Pat Faraway and I am the Director of Membership and Training for the Golf Mulligan Association. I am also a spokesperson for the millions of mulligan users, like you, worldwide. (This has got to be the best job on the planet. I am so excited for you.)

Becoming a member of the Association is as easy as using a foot wedge to relocate a ball from behind a tree. To become a member all you need to do is take the following steps:

Membership Qualification:

1. Receive psychological conditioning to reduce the guilt you might experience taking the mulligans,
2. Pass a quick, five question true or false quiz,
3. Recite the Association Pledge of Allegiance,
4. Learn the important secret handshake, and
5. Receive your membership certificate

Completing the qualification process takes only a short time. Then you can get out on the course, take advantage of the world class mulligans in this user's guide, and begin realizing dramatic improvements to your golf score and self-esteem.

Before starting the membership qualification activities, I would like to share a letter that I received from Chris Green. I met Chris at a golf store where I buy two dozen new golf balls every week.

The Chris Green Letter

Dear Pat,

Kelly Smith, my best friend, called me up on a Monday to ask me if I would like to go golfing the following Saturday. Kelly attended a golf outing and won a round of golf at The Meadows Country Club in the golf outing raffle. I just about fell off my chair! I was going to golf at The Meadows!

The Meadows is a private golf course. It is one of the stops on the tour and it is very, very exclusive. One of the members at The Meadows, Mr. Kensington, donated the round of golf to the outing. He is the president of a very successful and growing internet-based company in the area, and we would be golfing with him and a guest.

The opportunity to play at The Meadows was like a dream come true. I had never played on a professional quality course. Also, my background is in computer networking and the opportunity to meet an influential person like Mr. Kensington was very timely from a career standpoint.

My friend Kelly told me that it was important for me to have my best "country club" image going for Saturday. This meant upscale golf attire, a substantial golf bag, sharp head covers, name-brand golf balls, a fancy divot tool, a unique ball marker, and all the related accessories. Kelly also told me to bring some pretty serious cash, so that we could buy Mr. Kensington a few "beverages" and have dinner afterwards.

The week dragged on like I was living in slow motion. I thought that Saturday would never come. During the week I spent a small pile of money to bring myself up to "country club" standards. I also went to the driving range a few extra times. The golf clothes, accessories, extra driving range trips, and the entertainment funds for Saturday set me back about $400. But, I didn't care! I was golfing at The Meadows Country Club!

Saturday finally arrived. Kelly and I met at the clubhouse, checked in at the pro shop, and waited for Mr. Kensington. He arrived along with the last part of our foursome, his daughter Katie Kensington.

We had a couple of "beverages" at the clubhouse, got our golf carts, hit a few balls at the range, and then headed to the first tee. I was looking the part, the day was sunny and 70 degrees, and Mr. Kensington and I were getting along fabulously.

We arrived at the first tee and Mr. Kensington pulled out a tee and threw it up in the air a few times to determine the order in which we would tee off. It would be me, Mr. Kensington, Katie Kensington, and then my friend Kelly.

Mr. Kensington gave us the low-down on the first hole. It was a par four, dogleg right with no hazards. I was very, very nervous, but I stood up to the tee with confidence, took a nicely paced backswing, an equally well-paced downswing, and hit the ball. It went twenty-five feet, hit the forward tee marker, and went into the woods directly next to our tee box.

I would have gone into cardiac arrest from embarrassment. However, I simply walked over to my golf bag, pulled out my copy of World Class Mulligans, and turned to the page with the appropriate Association approved mulligan. I told my playing partners that I was a member of the Golf Mulligan Association and that I would now be taking a mulligan. To my pleasant surprise, Mr. Kensington said that he was also a member of the Association and that he would be using one or more of the world class mulligans during the round.

I want to thank the Golf Mulligan Association for making mulligans legal and for providing this handy Official User's Guide. My experience at The Meadows would have been much different if I had not been armed with it.

Six weeks later I got a job with Mr. Kensington's company. I am also engaged to his daughter; the lovely, six handicap Katie Kensington.

Best Regards,

Chris Green

It was so kind of Chris to share this heartwarming story with us because it means a lot to the people who read this guide.

We get hundreds of letters every year from our members around the globe like Chris Green. Regardless of country, language, golf course conditions, or slope ratings, there is one central theme in all of the letters. It is that their golf experiences would have been a lot different if they had not been a member of the Golf Mulligan Association.

Now, let's get back to the business of making you a member. As mentioned earlier, you need to go through a few brief steps to become a member. Then you can take this guide, go to the course, and begin improving your scores. The first thing we need to do is ensure that you have had the proper psychological conditioning to use the Association mulligans.

Psychological Conditioning

As a member of the Association, it is essential for you to have the strength and fortitude to use the Association approved mulligans without guilt or reservation. To make certain of this, we require that you learn five key Association fundamentals and take a five question quiz to determine if you understand the fundamentals. (Don't worry about passing the quiz. It's as easy as a ten foot "gimme" putt when you are playing a round of golf by yourself. Besides, we give you unlimited quiz mulligans to insure that you pass the quiz.)

Review the illustrations and participate in the exercises on the following pages that cover the five fundamentals. As you review each of the fundamentals you will notice a gradual, but significant, strengthening of your golf balls.

Fundamental #1

<u>It's Not the Same as Cheating</u>

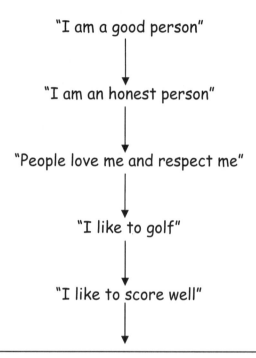

"I am a good person"

↓

"I am an honest person"

↓

"People love me and respect me"

↓

"I like to golf"

↓

"I like to score well"

↓

Countless rounds of golf, equipment purchases, lessons, practice range visits, and my golf game is still horrible.

↓

"I can use mulligans to improve my golf score"

Learning Point: To use a mulligan is not the same as cheating.

It's a Natural Part of Human Evolution

The mulligan is not a recent historical development. It is an integral part of the evolution of human beings and the tools needed to survive.

Rocks	Sticks	Fire	Excuses	Mulligans
5 million	2 million	700,000	30,000	1400

----------------- Years Ago ----------------

Learning Point: The mulligan is a natural part of human evolution.

Fundamental #3

It Will Not Conflict With Your Ethics

(Respond Yes or No - Please be very honest)

Do You Ever?   Yes   No

		Yes	No
1.	Roll your ball when it is not permitted	___	___
2.	Record one less stroke than you had on a hole	___	___
3.	Kick the ball from behind an obstacle	___	___
4.	Find another ball and use it instead of yours	___	___
5.	Drop a ball and claim it's your lost ball	___	___
6.	Say a complete miss was your practice swing	___	___
7.	Claim that someone must have hit your ball	___	___
8.	Test the sand by grounding the club head	___	___
9.	Make a noise to disturb your opponent	___	___
10.	Lie about your score for a round	___	___

If you answered Yes to one or more of the questions, you have a golf ethics level that will support using the mulligans in this guide.

Learning Point – There are many things that golfers routinely do that are much lower, ethically, than taking a mulligan.

Fundamental #4

It Has Deep Historical Roots

There are several versions of how the mulligan originated. Knowing the truth will give you strength. Try to determine which one of the following four stories is true.

(Please read carefully. Don't be deceived by completely ridiculous assertions and bad lies.)

1. David Mulligan, who played at the St. Lambert Country Club in Canada during the 1920's, would re-tee his ball after hitting an errant shot. His buddies dubbed it "A Mulligan".

2. Mulligan is a Scottish tavern word. Pat Mulligan, a tavern owner, would put a bottle of his newest scotch whiskey out for his patrons to take free shots. The free shots became known as mulligans. The term was later used in golf.

3. Golf originated in Scotland during the 15th century. At first, golfers could take a shot over if they didn't like it. The "take over" shot was named after the Isle of Mull, Scotland, a very difficult place to play golf. Retaking a shot was later banned by the better golfers.

4. A golf caddie during the 1930s named John A. "Buddy" Mulligan was known for encouraging golfers to replay shots they didn't like. He became a very popular caddie and the golfers at the course began calling any freebee shot "A Mulligan".

Learning Point - The mulligan was invented in 15th century Scotland and was originally part of the game of golf. (Story #3)

Fundamental #5

The End Justifies the Means

Examine the results of the first nine holes of play at The Meadows Country Club. What is the main point that you should take from these results?

The Meadows Country Club										
Hole	1	2	3	4	5	6	7	8	9	
Par	4	3	5	4	4	5	3	4	4	36
Chris Green	4	3	4	5	5	5	3	5	4	38
Ken Kensington	4	2	6	3	4	7	3	5	3	37
Katie Kensington	4	3	4	4	4	4	3	4	4	34
Kelly Smith	5	4	5	5	6	7	4	5	4	45

The main point you should take from the scorecard is that you must always be prepared with your Golf Mulligan Association world class mulligans. Chris, Ken and Katie are all members of the Association. Kelly Smith is not.

Learning Point - Always be prepared with your approved mulligans and have the extra balls to use them.

Membership Qualification Quiz
Association Fundamentals

		True	False
1.	To use a mulligan is not the same as cheating	___	___
2.	The mulligan is a natural part of human evolution	___	___
3.	There are many things that a golfer does that are much lower, ethically, than using a mulligan	___	___
4.	The mulligan was invented in 15th century Scotland and was originally part of the game of golf	___	___
5.	You should always be prepared with your world class mulligans and have the balls to use them	___	___

Answers – The answer to all five questions is True. If you answered False to any of the questions, you should go back and review the page relating to that fundamental. (There is no restriction on how many times you take the quiz. Remember you get unlimited quiz mulligans.) When you get the correct answers to all of the questions on the quiz, move on to the next page.

New Member Induction

If you made it this far in the guide, you have passed the membership qualification quiz and you are now positioned to become an official member of golf's greatest organization.

In the next few pages you will be officially inducted into the Association. You will:

- Recite the Pledge of Allegiance,
- Learn the secret handshake, and
- Receive your membership certificate

After this, Ben Whiffin, our Director of Mulligan Research, will introduce you to the approved and sanctioned Golf Mulligan Association world class mulligans.

Pledge of Allegiance
Golf Mulligan Association

Please read each of the lines below. Say these out loud and with enthusiasm:

- I have good intentions

- When I step up to the ball

- To hit it long and straight

- A "Fore" I do not want to call

- If I hit a wayward shot

- And end up in the clover

- I will proudly take a mulligan

- Hit 'em good or hit 'em over!

Now you can proceed to the next page and learn the Golf Mulligan Association's secret handshake.

Secret Handshake

It is important for you to know the secret handshake. When you meet another member of the Association they will greet you by secretly passing a golf ball to you while you are shaking hands.

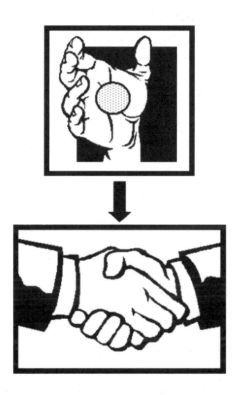

Please practice this handshake, so you will be prepared to use it whenever you meet another member.

Membership Certificate

We are very proud to award you the following exclusive certificate for successfully passing the challenging quiz, reciting the Pledge of Allegiance, and learning the member's secret handshake.

Golf Mulligan Association
Membership Certificate

On this day _____ (date)
_____ (name)
became a member of the Golf Mulligan Association. You must honor all requests by this individual to use any of the approved Association mulligans in this guide.

Hit 'em good or hit 'em over!

Moe Strokes - President

Make sure to fill in the certificate. This will help protect this valuable golf guide from thieves. Also, if you are requesting the use of one of the world class mulligans included in this guide and anyone challenges your membership, simply show them this distinctive, official certificate.

Warning

This is the second warning we have given you in this guide. The next section of the user's guide contains addictive material that can cause behavioral problems associated with golf. If you have a weak disposition or you are already having personal problems with golf, do not proceed to the next section.

The Basics

Director of Mulligan Research

Ben Whiffin

World Class Mulligans - The Basics

Hello! I am Ben Whiffin, Director of Mulligan Research for the Association. Now that you're a member, you can take advantage of the mulligans included in this guide. Beginning today you will have a distinct advantage on the golf course over non-member golfers.

What Is A World Class Mulligan?

A world class mulligan is when you take a golf shot over using a state-of-the-art, tested and proven, world class excuse.

By observing and listening to golfers during play, the Association determined that there were forty (40) different types of mulligans taken by golfers; each having a Beginner, Advanced, and Expert world class excuse for taking that type of mulligan. (As a note, during the research we also compiled the most comprehensive list of raunchy words and derogatory golf remarks. These may be the subject of a future publication.)

With forty mulligans and three different levels of excuses to take each mulligan, we had a whopping

120 world class mulligan opportunities. Doesn't that just make you tingle all over!

You might, at this point, ask what distinguishes a Beginner, Advanced, and Expert mulligan user. Our research indicates that an individual's ethics, outlook on humanity, level of intoxication, experience with the game, the quality of their sex life, and several other factors account for the differences.

After numerous dinner meetings and several boondoggles to the nation's finest golf resorts we voted on, and approved, the world class mulligans that are now a part of this groundbreaking guide. In a second vote, we declared golf mulligans legal in the game of golf. The rest is history.

Foreplay and Golf Orgies

The ways to use your world class mulligans are unlimited; ranging from basic golf foreplay to orgies.

- Foreplay – Take this guide to bed with you. Read through the mulligans and visualize yourself on the golf course with that warm feeling that comes from improving the outcome of your golf game by retaking your shots.

- <u>Playing with Yourself</u> – Play a round of golf by yourself and practice taking the mulligans on every shot. You will not experience the same gratification as when you are doing it with someone else, but you will still enjoy it very much.

- <u>Doing It With A Friend</u> – Take a few mulligans on the golf course in the intimate setting of just you and a friend. This is a great way to get experience and to get prepared for doing it with a group.

- <u>Foursomes</u> – Do it with three other people. Although some of you will be bashful about doing it with a group, you will eventually have to take your mulligans with a foursome.

- <u>Golf Orgies</u> – Give a copy of the guide to each foursome in your golf outing, or golf league, to use during competition.

Selecting the Correct Mulligan

There are two ways to use this guide. If you flub a shot and you are an experienced user of this guide, simply turn to the page containing the mulligan you want to deploy.

If, on the other hand, you have just started using the guide, simply thumb through the guide and pick a mulligan that sounds good. Don't worry about not finding one. There is a mulligan and supporting excuse to cover virtually every conceivable situation on the golf course.

Once you have made your selection, be prepared to present it to your playing partner(s).

Proper Etiquette Before Retaking Your Shot

The Golf Mulligan Association strongly supports etiquette in all aspects of the golf game. Using a mulligan is no exception.

When you want to use one of your world class mulligans, you need to inform your golf partner (or group) of your intent to use it by making the following statement:

"Pardon me. As you can see, my shot really sucked! I am a member of the Golf Mulligan Association and I will be retaking that shot. I will be using this Association approved, world class mulligan (show them the page in this guide) from the Official User's Guide."

If the members of your golf group react unfavorably and respond by rejecting your request, you can add the following additional language to your statement:

"I am not asking your permission to take a mulligan, simply telling you as a matter of courtesy."

If this is met with continued rejection, then you should add the following:

"Look you SOBs, I am hitting another ball. Get out of my way. I don't want to hit you in the head and ruin a perfectly good ball."

If this still doesn't work, then you will have to resort to one of the oldest tricks in the book. Simply offer to share your Official User's Guide on one of their shots.

Typical Score Improvements

The improvements in your score that you can realize from using your world class mulligans are far beyond what you can ever get from golf instruction, practicing, or otherwise improving your skills. The table on the following page illustrates the gains that can be achieved.

World Class Mulligans
Typical Score Improvements

Method	Maximum Stroke Reductions Per Round of Golf
first tee only	one stroke
one per round any hole	one stroke
one per nine	two strokes
one on each hole	eighteen strokes
whenever you want	whatever you need *
virtual golf round	guaranteed par **

Notes:

* Use unlimited mulligans to get your desired score (The preferred Association method).

** Don't play at all. Declare the use of unlimited mulligans and relax and have a few beverages.

Are you ready? Start your golf carts and tee up your balls because the next section of the guide contains the Golf Mulligan Association's approved world class mulligans.

Hit 'em good or hit 'em over! – Ben Whiffin

World Class Mulligans By Category

Personal Issues
Course Conditions
Golf Skills
Equipment

World Class Mulligans

Personal Issues

Confused

I am retaking my golf shot because:

Beginner

I thought this was a scramble

Advanced

I didn't know we were betting on this

Expert

You didn't tell me I had to keep score

Distracted

I am retaking my golf shot because:

Beginner

A member of my foursome made a distracting noise

Advanced

A celebrating foursome on the 11th green disturbed me

Expert

The voices in my head annoyed me

Alone Again

I am retaking my golf shot because:

Beginner

My spouse left me

Advanced

My sports psychologist moved
to another state

Expert

My golf instructor changed careers

Buzzed

I am retaking my golf shot because:

Beginner

I should not be drinking and golfing at the same time

Advanced

Eight beers in four holes is clouding my thinking

Expert

Burp! Wow man! I can dig it! How's about another golf shot?

Nervous

I am retaking my golf shot because:

Beginner

Playing with this "hottie" makes me
extremely nervous

Advanced

Playing with real golfers makes me
very anxious

Expert

Playing with myself is much
more satisfying

Sick

I am retaking my golf shot because:

Beginner

I have a headache

Advanced

I am feeling disoriented

Expert

I don't know who I am or what
I am doing here

Apprehensive

I am retaking my golf shot because:

Beginner

The 120 on my previous round has affected my confidence

Advanced

That 14 on the last hole has undermined my ability

Expert

The laughter throughout this round has destroyed my self esteem

Afraid

I am retaking my golf shot because:

Beginner

I hit a house and don't want to go
anywhere near it

Advanced

I hit a big dude and don't want to have
anything to do with him

Expert

I hit that dark forest and I am
scared to go in

Introverted

I am retaking my golf shot because:

Beginner

I don't like teeing off first

Advanced

I am not comfortable teeing off last

Expert

I have a severe case of delusional paranoid teephobia

Uninformed

I am retaking my golf shot because:

Beginner

It is not a dogleg right, like they said

Advanced

The course is not easy, like they said

Expert

I am not really a golfer, like I said

World Class Mulligans

Course Conditions

Tee Boxes

I am retaking my golf shot because:

Beginner

The tee box is wet and slippery

Advanced

I don't believe the tee boxes are regulation width

Expert

I got light-headed from the thin air on this elevated tee

Fairways

I am retaking my golf shot because:

Beginner

The fairway grass is too long

Advanced

The fairway has not been watered

Expert

The fairway has not been widened

Rough

I am retaking my golf shot because:

Beginner

The rough is too deep

Advanced

The rough is much too frequent

Expert

The rough is definitely not
Bermuda Northern grass

Bunkers

I am retaking my golf shot because:

Beginner

There are fairway bunkers in my sight

Advanced

Those tricky course designers have placed bunkers right near the green

Expert

There is an annoying bunker directly under my ball

Pin Placement

I am retaking my golf shot because:

Beginner

This is a difficult pin location

Advanced

This is not my favorite pin placement

Expert

The pin must be in a secret location

Hole Design

I am retaking my golf shot because:

Beginner

This cannot be a par three

Advanced

This cannot be a par four

Expert

This cannot be a par five

Ball Washers

I am retaking my golf shot because:

Beginner

There is no ball washer

Advanced

The ball washer is dry

Expert

The ball washer towel is a cotton and polyester blend

Wind

I am retaking my golf shot because:

Beginner

There was a sudden gust of wind during my backswing

Advanced

There was a pleasant, but challenging, northwesterly breeze during my downswing

Expert

There was an obnoxious breaking of the wind during my setup

Temperature

I am retaking my golf shot because:

Beginner

It is chilly out

Advanced

My game has cooled off

Expert

My balls are frozen

Light

I am retaking my golf shot because:

Beginner

The sun was in my eyes

Advanced

It is too dark out with these
sunglasses on

Expert

The hue and intensity of the sky is
making it ominous and threatening

World Class Mulligans

Golf Skills

Experience

I am retaking my golf shot because:

Beginner

I have only played executive par three
courses before today

Advanced

My only golf experience is a driving range
and a putt-putt golf course

Expert

This is much different than video golf

Shot Selection

I am retaking my golf shot because:

Beginner

I should have laid up, but didn't

Advanced

I tried to lay up, but couldn't

Expert

I need to get laid, but haven't

Aim

I am retaking my golf shot because:

Beginner

The tee box markers caused me to aim in the wrong direction

Advanced

That water hazard is much bigger than shown on the score card

Expert

My golf setup does not currently incorporate the aiming part

Muscle Memory

I am retaking my golf shot because:

Beginner

I should have warmed up at the range

Advanced

It takes me a few holes to warm up

Expert

I am afraid that my muscles have only
remembered the bad swings

Learning Ability

I am retaking my golf shot because:

Beginner

I hit the ball into the water

Advanced

I hit the ball into the water again

Expert

I hit the ??#@? ball into
the water again

Preparation

I am retaking my golf shot because:

Beginner

That miss was a practice swing

Advanced

That hit was a practice swing

Expert

That hit was a practice hit

Tee Box Selection

I am retaking my golf shot because:

Beginner

I play from the whites – we are playing
from the golds

Advanced

I play from the whites – we are playing
from the blues

Expert

I play from the blues – we are playing
from the whites

Club Selection

I am retaking my golf shot because:

Beginner

I used the wrong club

Advanced

I hit the right club wrong

Expert

I'm at the wrong club, right?

Practice

I am retaking my golf shot because:

Beginner

It was my first tee shot of the day

Advanced

That was my first tee shot on
the back nine

Expert

That was my first tee shot on this hole

Professional Training

I am retaking my golf shot because:

Beginner

I need to take some lessons

Advanced

I need an emergency session with my golf instructor

Expert

I think I should call 911

World Class Mulligans

Equipment

Clubs

I am retaking my golf shot because:

Beginner

My new big-headed driver is making me miss hit the ball

Advanced

This titanium, triple-ball, wide-faced, long-handled, curved putter does not connect the ball squarely

Expert

These new green golf club grips are not very user friendly

Balls

I am retaking my golf shot because:

Beginner

This ball is not my usual brand

Advanced

This is not my usual ball number

Expert

This unusual dimple pattern is resulting in what is called a "convex flux force migration vector"

Gloves

I am retaking my golf shot because:

Beginner

My glove has a hole in it

Advanced

This is not my usual glove color

Expert

My dog ate my golf glove

Head Covers

I am retaking my golf shot because:

Beginner

I accidentally put my driver head cover
on my three wood

Advanced

I had my nine iron head cover
on my six iron

Expert

I had my putter head cover
on my seven iron

Golf Clothes

I am retaking my golf shot because:

Beginner

My rain jacket is too "restrictive"

Advanced

My golf hat is too "snug"

Expert

My golf pants are too "tacky"

Golf Shoes

I am retaking my golf shot because:

Beginner

I forgot my golf shoes

Advanced

I am missing some spikes

Expert

I cannot get used to these wing-tips

Tees

I am retaking my golf shot because:

Beginner

I just started using these long tees

Advanced

My ball fell off this small tee and
dribbled out there 20 yards

Expert

These multi-colored bags of tees
are very confusing

Lost Items

I am retaking my golf shot because:

Beginner

I am missing some of my clubs

Advanced

I am missing a pencil with an eraser

Expert

I am missing several important golf skills

Golf Cart

I am retaking my golf shot because:

Beginner

I prefer to ride

Advanced

I prefer to walk

Expert

I prefer electric carts

Range Finders

I am retaking my golf shot because:

Beginner

This little $10.00 range finder is not worth a shit

Advanced

The distance markers on the course have been consistently wrong

Expert

The GPS on my cart must be old technology

Assistance for Mulligan and
Golf Addicts

Director of Member
Assistance

U.T. Upagain

Assistance for Mulligan and Golf Addicts

Hello, I am U.T. Upagain, Director of Member Assistance for the Association. If you have problems with addiction to mulligans or golf in general, this section of the guide provides assistance. The Association has turned to the principles of the Buddhist philosophy of life for our inspiration.

In 589 BC, Buddha Shakyamuni, founded Buddhism. The main goal of Buddhism is as follows:

<u>Lead all human beings to a permanent liberation from suffering</u>

For our members this means permanently eliminating the suffering from high scores, broken clubs, lost balls, lost money, and lost self-esteem due to continued exposure to the game of golf.

The central principles of Buddhism are demonstrated in **The Four Noble Truths and the Eight Steps to Enlightenment.**

By understanding these key principles you will be a more enlightened golfer. At a minimum, you will be a better person even if you remain a suffering golfer.

The Four Noble Truths

1. Life is filled with suffering
2. Desire for wealth, happiness, and other forms of selfish enjoyment cause suffering
3. Suffering will end with the elimination of desires
4. Eliminating desires will be achieved by following The Eight Step Path to Enlightenment.

Translation for Golf

You suffer from the game of golf. The suffering comes from your desire to have a single digit handicap and to hear them yell "you da man" or "you go girl". You know you will never achieve this, yet you persist. Your suffering will only be eliminated when you purge yourself of this desire using The Eight Step Path to Enlightenment.

The Eight Step Path to Enlightenment

1. <u>One must accept the Four Noble Truths.</u>

   You must accept that you are suffering, that your golf score will never improve, that everyone else knows it, and that you must purge yourself of the desire to achieve that unattainable goal.

2. <u>One must eliminate all desires and thoughts of lust, bitterness, and cruelty; and must harm no living creature.</u>

   Stop lusting for a 78. Don't be bitter when you shoot a 110. Stop all cruel thoughts of harming your golf instructor and throwing your clubs in a lake.

3. <u>One must speak only truth. There can be no slander, lying, or vain talk.</u>

   Don't accuse others of cheating. Don't lie about your golf scores or handicap. Abstain from bragging and being puffy about your occasional success on the course.

4. <u>One must abstain from sexual immorality, stealing, and killing of any kind.</u>

Refrain from making off-color sexual remarks and ogling or groping members of the opposite sex on the golf course. Don't steal (strokes, beers, golf balls) or hit others with errant shots.

5. <u>One must work in an occupation that benefits others and harms no one.</u>

Get a sales job or similar job that eliminates your need to make lame excuses in order to go to the golf course.

6. <u>One should seek to attain good and moral qualities and develop those already possessed.</u>

You can give this one a try, but it is not possible for most golfers to comply with this one.

7. <u>One must be observant, contemplative, and free of desire and sorrow.</u>

Observe the behavior of good golfers, reflect on your successes, and don't whine and continuously talk about how you could have done better if the equipment was newer, the greens were firmer, the temperature was cooler, and the beer was tastier.

8. <u>Practice meditation so that you can overcome any sensation of pleasure and pain.</u>

Have a few "beverages" until your head is so numb that you forget your problems and you reach a state of nirvana.

If you read and practice the Eight Steps you should be able to move forward without suffering from golf or mulligan addiction. If you are not able to get any benefit out of this, then you are probably beyond help.

Hit 'em good or hit 'em over! – U.T. Upagain

Paring Remarks
By President Moe Strokes

Well, that wraps it up. You have received your training and you have become a member of the Association. Now you can go to the golf course and use the approved mulligans included in this guide.

We would like to thank you for joining our fine organization, and let you know that we couldn't be any prouder of you – our new best friend. As a parting request, please be sensitive to the other non-member golfers who don't have access to the Association approved mulligans. They are at a distinct disadvantage.

If you ever feel that you are losing your nerve to use the advanced or expert mulligans in this guide, please repeat the psychological conditioning section of the guide. Likewise, if you find yourself obsessing over mulligans, or golf in general, please review the information in the section on assistance for addicts.

Good luck in all of your golf and life endeavors.

Hit 'em good or hit 'em over! – Moe Strokes

About the Author

Glenn Rader (a.k.a. Andy Parzit) is a writer and avid golfer who lives in Michigan. He is the president of NooVoo LLC, a product innovation and development company. He has an MBA from the University of Michigan.

Glenn is surrounded by nineteen golf courses and six golf equipment supply stores in his area. At one time he was a frustrated 14 handicap golfer. He created the fictitious Golf Mulligan Association, declared mulligans legal, and published World Class Mulligans. He is now a scratch golfer.

Help Me. Please!

Struggling
and
Desperate
Golfer

To purchase additional copies of
<u>World Class Mulligans</u> visit:

www.WorldClassMulligans.com

This book is available at quantity discounts